SERIES EDITOR
EOIN PURCELL

Irish Heroes for Children
THE STORY OF
DANIEL O'CONNELL

ULTAN MACKEN

MERCIER PRESS
WHAT YOU NEED TO READ

MERCIER PRESS
Cork
www.mercierpress.ie

Trade enquiries to CMD Distribution
55A Spruce Avenue, Stillorgan Industrial Park, Blackrock, Co. Dublin

© Ultan Macken, 1975
This edition 2008

ISBN: 978 1 85635 596 4
10 9 8 7 6 5 4 3 2 1

A CIP record for this title is available from the British Library

In the extracts from other works quoted here we have occasionally altered a word or a phrase where we felt the original would have been beyond the comprehension of the young reader – Editor.

Mercier Press receives financial assistance from the Arts Council/An Chomhairle Ealaíon

This book is sold subject to the condition that it shall not, by way of trade or otherwise, be lent, resold, hired out or otherwise circulated without the publisher's prior consent in any form of binding or cover other than that in which it is published and without a similar condition including this condition being imposed on the subsequent purchaser.

No part of this publication may be reproduced or transmitted in any form or by any means, electronic or mechanical, including photocopying, recording or any information or retrieval system, without the prior permission of the publisher in writing.

Printed and bound in the EU

CONTENTS

Preface 7
Morgan O'Connell's New Son 9
Going to School 14
The French Revolution 20
Studying Law in England 23
Daniel Returns to Ireland 29
Castlereagh 40
Speaking Against the Union 44
Secret Marriage 47
The Catholic Committee 51
The *Evening Post* 57
The Duel 68
Sir Robert Peel 72
The Reawakening of the Irish Nation 76
The Election 83
Emancipation 87
A Second Election 89
Workhouses 102

The Last Campaign 105
The Nation 108
Imprisonment 117
The Great Famine 122
The Last Journey 125

Preface

Irish history is packed with figures of amazing ability who lived lives that seem straight out of storybooks. Names like Michael Collins and Éamon de Valera might need no introduction, but what of the other patriots – Henry Grattan, Robert Emmet, Arthur Griffith and Isaac Butt? Even our folklore is full of heroes; Fionn Mac Cumhaill, Cúchulainn and Maeve of Connaught are more than characters from stories. All these people's lives tell us about ourselves and our country.

Drawing on some of the most talented Irish writers, we hope to open up the lives of our mythic and more recent heroes. The goal is to make the stories as accessible as possible to young readers. Over time the series will build into an invaluable set of mini-biographies that casts light on who the Irish are and where we have come from.

Eoin Purcell

Morgan O'Connell's New Son

On the morning of 6 August 1775, Morgan O'Connell came into his wife Catherine's bedroom to see his first son, who had just been born. He had decided to call him Daniel, after his own father, Donal Mór. I can see Morgan, who was to father nine more children, leaving his wife with the baby in her arms and going into the front room, where he stood in front of a log fire. He was worried about what was going to happen to his son when he grew up, as few careers were open to Catholics at that time. Even a landowner like Morgan O'Connell had very few rights.

Life went on as usual in the house at Carhen in Co. Kerry. The baby, however, did not stay long with his parents. The average Irish house at that time was so small that a custom had grown up among landowners of sending their children to spend their early years in labourers' houses. Still an infant, Daniel was sent to be mothered by the wife of one of Morgan's shepherds. For his first four years, he thought that his foster parents were his real parents. He spoke only Irish, and he lived in a small cottage.

A labourer's cottage in those days was very small. It often had no window because there was a tax on windows. Sometimes it had no chimney. The door was made in two pieces. The bottom half remained closed most of the time and kept out the hens. The top half was left open, letting in light and letting out smoke. The floor was solid rock or hard, dry clay that was warmer under the feet. The roof was thatched – just as some Irish cottages are roofed to this day. In one corner was a large bed that often consisted of no more than a large mattress of clean straw. There was very little other furniture. Food was cooked in large iron pots over a fire lit in the middle of the floor.

When Morgan O'Connell brought his son home to Carhen for a visit, he spoke to him in Irish, for Daniel understood no other language. Once, when Morgan asked him if he was getting enough to eat, Daniel replied: 'Oh yes. Dad brought in one of Morgan O'Connell's sheep and killed it.'

Morgan was still concerned about his son's future,

but his worries were soon over. His unmarried brother Maurice suggested adopting Daniel, who would come to live at his home in Derrynane and become his heir.

So Daniel left his foster parents and went to his uncle Maurice at Derrynane, where he was to live until he was fifteen. His uncle's house was the only one in the district with a slate roof. Its back was to the sea and it faced a walled courtyard planted with trees. It was three storeys and there were out-houses, kitchens and servants' quarters. The halls had two magnificent gold-edged mirrors from France, and the cellars were full of French and Spanish wines.

Daniel found that his uncle's riches did not come, as he had thought, from working the land, but from trading and smuggling. He, and merchants like him, made good use of the 120,000 'Wild Geese' who had left Ireland between 1690 and 1730. They acted as agents in France and Spain.

Ireland in those times exported cattle, hides and wool on a large scale. These were legal exports, but there was also a huge market for illegal salt, not only in France and Spain, but also in Scotland and England. Daniel's uncle had his own salt caves along the bay known as the Kenmare River. Local people worked in these salt caves and in his uncle's tanneries.

Maurice O'Connell had built up such a trade that he was able to maintain his own ships. Because he lived in a remote part of west Kerry, he could safely import many illegal goods from the continent – silk, lace, textiles, wines and spirits, tobacco, sugar and tea. He had a distinct hatred for taxes, as was clearly shown by the small velvet hat he wore. Most of the Catholic gentry wore beaver hats, but when the English introduced a tax on these, Maurice changed to the velvet one. He was then nicknamed 'Maurice an Chaipín', or 'Hunting Cap'.

Young Daniel noticed other remarkable things in his new home. There was a rough chapel where the people of the area went to Mass openly on Sundays. And his uncle and the household usually spoke English, using Irish only with the poor.

Maurice O'Connell thought his nephew's prospects were dim. Many anti-Catholic laws, or Penal Laws, were still in force. Introduced in 1692, they prohibited Catholics from going into Parliament, from going abroad for education, from owning horses of greater value than £5, and from having public schools in Ireland. Catholics were not allowed to purchase land, though they could inherit it from other Catholics. But even such Catholic estates as existed had to be

Many anti-Catholic laws, or Penal Laws, were still in force

divided among all the sons of a family unless the eldest became a Protestant. Catholics were forbidden to vote, excluded from careers in law and the army, and were barred from juries. With such laws in force, Daniel's uncle could see only two possible careers for his young nephew – as a soldier in the Irish Brigade in France or as a merchant acting for him either in France or in Ireland.

Going to School

Whatever happened, Maurice was determined that his nephew would get a good education, and Daniel was sent to study under a master named David O'Mahoney at a local hedge school. Education of any kind was hard to come by in those days. There were no Catholic schools, and the Church would not allow children to go to any others. Illegal schools sprang up and were called hedge schools – not because they were always held under a hedge but because they had no permanent building. Sometimes, class was held in a barn, an out-house or a kitchen. Sometimes, in summer, it was held in the shade of a hedge. The masters travelled a lot, and were paid either a very small amount of money or else with food and their keep. They taught a wide range of subjects, but mainly English, arithmetic, Latin and religion.

Daniel O'Connell first went to this kind of school, in Derrynane, at the age of four. Even at that early age, he was a quick learner, and even memorised the alphabet in an hour. Although he believed he was naturally lazy, he had a driving desire to be better than the other children, and for that reason worked very hard.

As a child, he loved the beauty of his country. He loved the mountains and the sea. He felt a closeness to famous Irishmen of long ago, and he felt that before he died he would like to do something for his country. Meanwhile, he enjoyed himself in Derrynane. He was very fond of reading, often going off by himself to read books while his friends were playing.

... he would like to do something for his country

The next step for Daniel was to continue his education in a school in France. He and his uncle Maurice were relying on the influence of another uncle, Colonel Daniel O'Connell – who was in the Irish Brigade in France – to get Dan and his brother Maurice to France.

By May of 1788 trouble was brewing in France. The king and all royalty were losing favour, as were the Irish Brigade and its officers. Colonel O'Connell wrote to his brother saying that he was not sure that France was the right place to send his young nephews. By the following year, trouble had in fact broken out, and though the colonel was even more reluctant, he found a suitable school in France – the college of St Omer.

In January 1790 he recommended that the two boys should not be sent 'until the present clouds go away'. The boys, very disappointed, were instead sent in the spring to a new Catholic school run by Father Harrington in Little Island near Cork. At the end of the year, despite the colonel's continuing warnings, the boys were sent to France; Daniel was fifteen.

They travelled by boat, first from Cork to Dover and then from Dover to Ostend; from there, they went by horse-drawn coach to St Omer. Anti-English feeling was very strong in France then. On the coach journey, a Frenchman ranted and raved about the English. He was angry when he found that he could not get the two young Irishmen to attack England in the same way. Daniel told him that as an Irishman he had no more affection for England than had the French.

It was January 1791 when the two boys began their studies at the famous school of St Omer. They studied five basic subjects – Latin, Greek, French, English and geography – and learned music, dancing, fencing and drawing. Daniel did well, coming second in his class in Latin, Greek and English, but only eleventh in French. His headmaster, Dr Stapleton, sent an encouraging recommendation home to his uncle Maurice: 'Unless I am very much mistaken,' he wrote, 'this boy is destined to be a remarkable figure in society.'

'this boy is destined to be a remarkable figure in society'

But Daniel's younger brother Maurice had not been doing as well at St Omer, and their uncle, the colonel, did not like the emphasis in the college on languages. He favoured mathematics, logic and rhetoric. But the colonel was very busy, and Daniel found a different school for them, Douai College. He wrote to tell the colonel, and the two boys moved to Douai in August 1792. There, they began to study new subjects such as rhetoric and philosophy.

In September Daniel announced in one of his letters home that he was going to study to become a barrister. A legal career would not have been open to him as a Catholic, but the French and American revolutions had frightened the English government. It felt that it had better try to win the loyalty of its Catholic subjects so a Catholic Relief Act was introduced in England in 1791. It allowed Catholics entry into the army and the professions, recognised the rights of Catholics to have their own worship in public, and allowed them to set up their own schools.

Though an English Catholic Committee had this Relief Act passed quite easily in England, there was no such Act for Ireland. But Irish Catholics had become hopeful, and the Irish Catholic Committee began to grow in strength. A leading Catholic merchant named John Keogh began to organise opposition to the anti-Catholic laws in a peaceful way. During 1792, a brilliant young man began to help the Committee – his name, Theobald Wolfe Tone.

Frightened by the growth of the Catholic Committee, the Irish Parliament, which was entirely Protestant, passed the Catholic Relief Act in the spring of 1792. This allowed Catholics to go into the professions, the army and the navy, and gave legal recognition to Catholic worship. However, Catholics were still denied the vote.

Catholics were still denied the vote

The Catholic Committee had gained so much it would not give up. Towards the end of 1792, it held a conference of Catholics from all over Ireland. They wanted 'emancipation'. A delegation saw the king, and he went over the head of the Irish Parliament and granted the vote to certain landowners, together with the right to sit on juries. The Irish Parliament was forced to carry through these reforms in January 1793.

The French Revolution

Because of these events at home, Daniel could now think of taking up a career as a barrister. At Douai, fees were not high at twenty-five guineas a year, but he disliked the living conditions – he complained that they received very small portions at dinner, and had to pay for their own washing.

The fortunes of Colonel O'Connell, had taken a turn for the worse during the summer the boys moved from St Omer to Douai. He had fled from France and joined the British army as an ordinary soldier. He took part in the Battle of Valmy in September 1792, where the French revolutionaries defeated the British.

The French forces followed this victory with another a month later at Jem-appes, only thirty-six miles from Douai. The boys began to meet French troops when they went for walks. The soldiers shouted insults at them, calling them 'little Jesuits, little Capuchins'.

By January of 1793, when the boys had been only six months in Douai, it was obvious that the revolutionary troops were going to take over all religious houses, including their school. On 21 January the two boys left the school, taking with them very few of their belongings.

Daniel O'Connell was now a fine, powerfully built man of eighteen, with fluent French. His Catholic schooling had given him no sympathy for the revolutionaries. They were preparing to wage war on religion, and they had horrified the world with their executions. The boys were worried that they would be mistaken for young Englishmen if stopped, so they wore tricolour cockades on their hats to protect themselves.

On their coach journey, they were sometimes stopped by revolutionary troops who banged on the coach and shouted insults at them, but finally they reached Calais and got on the first boat for England. They heard then that the day they had left Douai, the king of France had been brought to the guillotine by the revolutionaries. On hearing this, they took the tricolour cockades from their hats and threw them into the sea. Fishermen picked up the cockades and cursed the two young men for insulting the revolution.

Two Irishmen joined them on board – the Sheares

brothers – and they were full of excitement. They had come from Paris, where they had witnessed the execution of the king. They had bribed one of the National Guards to dip a large handkerchief in the blood of the king, and this they now showed to the two O'Connell boys. A passenger asked the Sheares brothers how they could have endured such a terrible scene. But they replied that it was all for the 'cause'. They were members of Wolfe Tone's Society of United Irishmen. (The Sheares brothers were executed for their part in the rebellion of 1798.)

... they had witnessed the execution of the king

This bloodstained handkerchief and the events of the French Revolution made a lasting impression on Daniel, who would try to lead millions of Irish people to a bloodless victory.

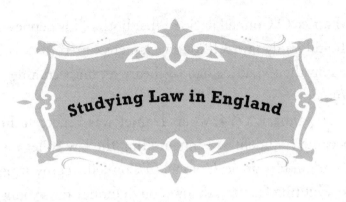

Studying Law in England

The O'Connell brothers arrived in England with hardly any belongings, but Colonel O'Connell found them lodgings and a new school. But they had not left the French Revolution behind. In England, they met exiles from France – either priests or friends of their uncle's. They told the boys that more and more people were going to the guillotine every day. Two months after they had left France, the O'Connell brothers heard that Douai College had been taken over by revolutionary troops, who seized all their personal belongings, including Daniel's violin.

Back in Ireland, their uncle Maurice's position had improved. Because of the new Catholic Relief Act of 1793, brought about by the visit of the Catholic Committee's delegation to King George III, he had been appointed deputy-governor of Kerry and a magistrate. This improved the boys' prospects, and

Maurice O'Connell decided that both of his nephews should study law. Although Daniel wanted to do so, his brother Maurice had his heart set on becoming a soldier.

In January 1794, when Daniel was nineteen, he became a student at Lincoln's Inn, the law college in London. His uncle, Colonel O'Connell, kept writing to 'Hunting Cap' to ask for enough money for a young law student in London. He said the very least Daniel could live on was £120 per year.

In the summer of 1795 Daniel made his first visit home to Derrynane. It took almost a fortnight to travel from London to west Kerry in those days. His uncle Maurice, having grown old and cranky, was not very glad to see him. He thought his young nephew was too lighthearted, and spent too much time chasing hares, foxes and otters. His young nephew's visit cost the old man too much, he thought. Daniel even borrowed his uncle's favourite horse. And what bothered him most was Daniel's new leaning towards the modern ideas of the French Revolution.

The colonel had also noticed this change in his nephew. He had thought that Daniel's nearness to the bloody results of the French Revolution while in school in Douai would prevent it. But both the colonel and

'Hunting Cap' were blind to the enthusiastic support that new democratic ideas were finding throughout Europe.

Even members of the British Parliament were talking about the new principles of 'Liberty, Equality and Fraternity'. A member of the House of Lords shocked guests at a dinner by proposing a toast not just to the king but also to the people, as 'Our Sovereign the People'.

... principles of 'Liberty, Equality and Fraternity'

Other influences were at work in the young law student's mind. He saw how poorly the British treated his uncle, the colonel, who had hoped the English would allow him to form an Irish brigade to attack the French revolutionary forces. But he came to realise that exiled Irishmen would never be allowed to fight in Europe in an organised way. (In August 1794 the British government decided that though an Irish regiment *would* be formed, it would only be allowed to serve in the West Indies. A year later, the colonel went off to serve with this regiment. He lasted only two years before dying of fever.) Daniel also saw how his brother Maurice's ambition to join the army was affected by the changing fortunes of the colonel. And he saw that Catholics, despite the Relief Acts, were still not free. He realised that they would still have to struggle to get their rights. Even a legal career was limited for a Catholic. Daniel could never become a senior barrister or a judge. These influences began to make the young man very different politically from his parents and from his uncles.

He had joined a debating society, the Honourable Society of Codgers in 1794, where new ideas such as human liberty and freedom of the press were discussed enthusiastically. There were many Irishmen in this society, and Daniel began to speak at its public meetings.

He began to keep a diary, and in it he criticised himself for spending too much time at the Codgers' Club. He wrote that he was lazy, not working, coming in late and not getting up in the morning until ten or eleven. He thought his uncle would not approve of this kind of life, and decided to move out of London to be away from all its distractions.

He found lodgings at Walpole House in Chiswick, beside the Thames. It was mostly a house for older people, and he thought it highly suitable. He wrote home to his uncle 'Hunting Cap', explaining why he had gone there:

> *I delayed answering your letter until I should have in my power to tell you that I changed my residence in accordance with your wishes. I am now only four miles from town, I pay the same price for board and lodgings as I should in London, but I enjoy many advantages here besides air and retirement. The society in this house is mixed, composed of men and women, all of rank and knowledge of the world, so that their conversation and manners are well adapted to rub off the rust of scholastic education. There is no danger of riot or dissipation, as they are all advanced in life, another young student of law [Richard Bennet] and I being the only young people in the house.*

Walpole House and its occupants were an education in themselves, as Daniel's diary reveals. The landlady, Mrs Rigby, was ugly and strong-minded, with an excellent memory. She spoke Italian and French, read Latin, and knew an enormous amount about the theatre. Daniel spent a lot of time arguing with her about new plays and about new thinking being promoted in modern books. Many of these books were political, as is obvious from their titles: *Decline and Fall*, *The Age of Reason*, *The Rights of Man* and *The Manual of Liberty*.

Daniel read and studied the writings of people such as Voltaire, Paine and Rousseau.

He went to many parties, and became very friendly with Richard Bennet. Daniel had been studying law in London for two years, and had learned a lot since leaving Douai. His mind was now made up on many fundamental things. He regarded personal liberty as the most important right, and held this belief until he died.

In 1796 Daniel left London and came back to Ireland to study at the King's Inns in Dublin.

Daniel Returns to Ireland

Daniel had come to Dublin just two years before the 1798 rebellion. The Catholic Committee had disbanded once the Catholic Relief Act was passed in 1793. In that same year, a new viceroy, Lord Fitzwilliam, had taken office. He was pro-Catholic, and there were great hopes that he would bring about full Catholic emancipation. But the British government refused to support a bill for Catholic emancipation that Henry Grattan put through the Irish Parliament. Lord Fitzwilliam resigned, and Lord Camden was appointed in his place in March 1795.

While these changes had been happening, the revolutionary Society of United Irishmen had been growing. They did not want to merely reform the existing Irish Parliament, but sought to break the connection with England and set up an Irish republic. They hoped that France would send some troops over to help them. In 1794 the United Irishmen were mostly Protestants, mainly from the north of the country. Wolfe Tone, their leader, wanted to change that, and he helped the Catholic Committee in its campaign for rights.

He felt that the smouldering resentments of the poorer Catholics against landlords and tithes could help him. But a threat to his ideal of unifying Catholics and poor Protestants was growing – the threat of fighting between the two that had been growing in Ulster from 1790. The trouble was over possession of land. There was rapid growth in population and therefore a great demand for land. Protestant farmers wanting to take land from Catholics formed armed bands called Peep o' Day Boys. They raided Catholic farms and demanded that the Catholics leave. Catholics had similar armed bands, called Defenders.

The arrival in March 1795 of the new viceroy, Lord Camden, did not reduce the sectarian hatred. Lord Camden decided that it would be more sensible for young Irishmen to train as priests in Ireland than on the continent, so Maynooth College was established. But this still did not satisfy all Catholics, and many turned to the Society of United Irishmen.

The sectarian troubles worsened in the north: in September the Defenders were badly beaten by the Peep o' Day Boys in a pitched battle. That night, the Protestants formed a new society to protect themselves: the Orange Society. The Orangemen began persecuting Catholics living in Armagh. Thousands of Catholic farmers fled to Connacht. Many more joined the Defenders. The United Irishmen continued to encourage Catholics to join with them.

The government in Dublin was becoming alarmed, especially since the arrest of a French agent in Dublin in April 1794. Some members of the United Irishmen were frightened at the thought of rebellion, and they fled from Ireland to the continent.

The government in Dublin was becoming alarmed

Wolfe Tone himself came to an agreement with the British government by confessing his role with the United Irishmen, and the English set him free and allowed him to go to America in May 1795. Tone did not stay long in America. By January 1796, he was in Paris actively seeking help from the French government.

The United Irishmen in Ireland continued to prepare for an uprising, and the British government decided to crack down on them. An Insurrection Act was passed, and it gave great powers to the authorities. Anyone convicted of administering an unlawful oath could be hanged. The viceroy could declare any district 'disturbed'. In such a district, magistrates could search anywhere for arms, and could send suspected persons to jail or to serve in the fleet. The Irish Parliament passed the Insurrection Act with only the minimum amount of discussion. The Irish parliamentarians were frightened by the threat of a rising, and would have agreed to anything that would restore law and order. In September 1796 a civilian army was recruited. It was called the Yeomen, or militia.

This was the disturbed condition of Daniel O'Connell's country when he returned to study law at the King's Inns in Dublin in the autumn of 1796. He settled into a good solid routine of work. Attendance at the King's Inns meant merely going to a certain number of dinners there with older barristers. It was felt that the young students would learn about law from conversations at these dinners. But O'Connell was not satisfied with merely sitting down to dinners. He joined the Dublin library and worked there from early morning until it closed at ten o'clock at night. Every time he read a book, he would write an extensive criticism of it.

He was happy in his lodgings. Indeed, he felt a little too happy and wondered if there were sad days ahead. He joined another debating society, the Historical Society, and there made friends. He also met again his old friend from London, Richard Bennet, who had married some months previously. His meeting with Bennet finally brought O'Connell into contact with the Society of United Irishmen, as Bennet belonged to its directorate. O'Connell joined, but his heart did not seem to be in it.

Events in Ireland were coming to a head. In December 1796 news came to Dublin that Wolfe Tone had arrived in Bantry Bay with 6–7,000 French troops. Bad weather and disagreement among the commanders prevented the force from landing, but both the British government and the ruling Irish Parliament were frightened. The government decided to attack the centres of rebellion in the country. The north was first, for Belfast was the most active centre of revolutionary feeling. The United Irishmen there had started a newspaper in 1791 – the *Northern Star* – in which they promoted the theories of the French Revolution and sought to revive the ancient Irish nation. They also promoted Irish poetry, music and literature.

The government sent General Lake into Ulster. Houses were burned. Suspected persons were tortured or flogged to find out the whereabouts of arms. The printing works of the *Northern Star* was burned to the ground. Thousands of muskets and pikes were captured. Many thousands of people took the oath of allegiance to the crown to avoid being tortured or killed.

This attack on the United Irishmen was effective. Very few people working for an uprising were left in Ulster. The great majority of northern Presbyterians who had been United Irishmen lost heart, and were now content to wait for reforms.

... people took the oath of allegiance to the crown to avoid being tortured or killed

The government oppression continued. Armed bands of Defenders in Leinster and Munster were brutally put down, though they still remained active, attacking places where they could get arms, and people who, they felt, supported the government. The numbers who supported the United Irishmen were still large – 110,000 in Ulster, 100,000 in Munster and 68,000 in Leinster.

O'Connell, meanwhile, was flirting with both sides. He followed the example of many of his student friends and joined the lawyers' branch of the Yeomanry. He liked the look of himself in the scarlet-and-blue uniform. At the same time, he continued his reading and felt sympathy for the United Irishmen. However, he did not want to go to jail, and when he attended the meetings of the Society of United Irishmen in Eustace Street, he was careful about what he said. Many people were being arrested, and he did not want to be among them.

In 1797 he felt it would be sensible to leave Dublin for a while. He spent the summer in Derrynane with his uncle 'Hunting Cap', who disapproved both of his politics and of his inability to drink as much as he himself could. 'Hunting Cap' thought it disgraceful that his nephew could not drink more than three glasses of wine and stay sober. He knew that his nephew disapproved of his custom of sending his guests home drunk.

O'Connell was being watched closely by informers.

One of them, the sham squire Francis Higgins, reported to Dublin Castle that O'Connell held a commission with the French army, that he was to be called to the bar to please a rich old uncle, and that he was a bloodthirsty revolutionary. Though he did not know he was being watched, O'Connell must have realised the danger of not being called to the bar, so he called upon a government official said to be pro-Catholic. He found that this man was in despair, as he feared that hatred against Catholics had become so great that they might lose the privileges they had already gained. But O'Connell was lucky: he was formally called to the bar on 26 April 1798. And he took the oath of allegiance to the crown.

The United Irishmen were planning their rebellion, and the government heard about most of their plans from informers and spies. In March 1798 they arrested most of the leaders. One escaped – Lord Edward Fitzgerald – and with his help the remainder of the organisation planned the uprising for 23 May. But just four days before that date, the government arrested Lord Edward. He died from wounds received during his arrest.

The uprising took place, but in a very disorganised way because the leaders were gone. Only in Wexford – under Father Murphy – did the rebels have any chance. They defeated a large force of north Cork militia, and soon had almost all of Co. Wexford in their hands. Having taken over the towns of Wexford and Enniscorthy, they attacked New Ross on 5 June.

... the government heard about most of their plans from informers and spies

The government commander had only 1,400 troops – all militia. The rebels attacked for twelve hours, before growing tired. When the government troops attacked, the rebels were forced to flee, many dying on the retreat. The Wexford rebels were finally defeated on Vinegar Hill on 21 June. Widespread destruction followed. Houses were burned and the inhabitants who had anything to do with the rebels were executed.

In Ulster, Henry Joy McCracken in Co. Antrim and Henry Munro in Co. Down led armed men against the government in Antrim and Ballynahinch. But within ten days, the insurrection in Ulster was over. McCracken and Munro were executed with some of the other leaders, but the rest of the rebels were freed. The rebellion in Ulster was mostly a Protestant one. There were far more Catholics in the militia than among the rebels. The opposite was true in Wexford.

Success in the uprising had depended on the landing of French troops. None came until 22 August, when 1,100 men under General Humbert landed at Killala, Co. Mayo. Humbert was amazed that there was no rising in Connacht, and that large numbers of Irishmen did not join his army. But he was a clever fighter and managed to beat a large force of militia under General Lake at Castlebar. He fought on until 8 September, and after the French forces' surrender, the militia took its revenge on the people of Connacht, plundering and killing.

Wolfe Tone had meanwhile set out from France with another force of French soldiers, but they were captured off Donegal by the British navy. Tone was captured, brought to Dublin, tried by court martial, and condemned to death. He asked that he be shot, not hanged. When this request was refused, he committed suicide in prison.

Daniel O'Connell had a strange summer. At the outbreak of the uprising, he was called up as a member of the lawyers' militia. He was posted on one of the canal bridges in Dublin to watch for any escaping rebels. He was given orders to shoot anyone he saw out after dark, but he allowed at least one group of his countrymen to escape, and he saved another man's life by putting his gun barrel in the path of a sword about to strike him.

That summer, O'Connell decided that Dublin was no place for a barrister who was both a revolutionary and a Yeoman. He sailed on a potato boat to Cork, and from there he made his way by road to Kerry – not to Derrynane, but to his father's house at Carhen. More news about the uprising reached him. There had been trials and executions; men were in jail, more were banished or had been sent as convicts to Botany Bay. Others had gone to serve the king of Prussia.

It was a sad summer. On one of his hunting trips, he caught a chill that kept him in bed and brought him close to death. But soon it was autumn, and he would soon start his career as a Catholic barrister in the courts throughout Ireland.

Castlereagh

Lord Cornwallis replaced Lord Camden as viceroy in June 1798, at the beginning of the uprising. He wished to make Ireland peaceful by governing well rather than through military terrorism. The uprising gave the British prime minister, William Pitt, the opportunity he was looking for: to unite Great Britain and Ireland, and abolish the Irish Parliament in Dublin. He appointed Robert Stewart (Lord Castlereagh) – an Irishman from Co. Derry – as chief secretary under Cornwallis, and told him to use every means to bring about a union under one parliament in London.

Pitt felt that the support of the Catholics was necessary to bring about the union. He understood that most Catholics were not lovers of a Protestant Irish Parliament, and he felt that if he promised full Catholic emancipation in return for supporting the union, he could get them behind the campaign. He also knew that the Catholic leaders – notably the Church hierarchy – disliked the violent means of the United Irishmen, and that they felt peace would come if Catholic emancipation were achieved. Pitt also told his chief secretary that he had to win over a majority in the Irish Parliament. Simply bribing with money and titles those who might vote against the proposed union could do this.

Lord Castlereagh began work in 1798. He approached the ten trustees of Maynooth College and told them that if Catholics supported the union, once it came into force Catholic emancipation would follow. If the Irish Parliament remained in existence, there would be no question of any relief for Catholics.

The bishops put their full weight behind obtaining the union throughout the country. Bishop Moylan of Cork approached Daniel O'Connell's uncle 'Hunting Cap'; he thought it was an excellent idea. In the same way, Archbishop Troy of Dublin received support from Catholics there.

Lord Castlereagh and Lord Cornwallis were satisfied with this new Catholic support, and they turned to the Members of Parliament. Bribes and promises of government office were offered in return for a vote for the union. Members who refused to support government policy were sacked from government jobs. The Speaker, Mr Foster – a prominent opponent of the union – could not be sacked, but his son, who held a job in the Revenue office, was.

By the end of 1798, Castlereagh and Cornwallis were confident that the union would get an easy passage through the Irish Parliament when it met on 22 January 1799. Although the government did not want to debate the issue on the opening day, the opposition members forced it to. The debate raged all that day and all night, and no vote was taken until the following afternoon. The government won, but only by one vote – 106 to 105. It was not happy with this result, and two days after the opening of Parliament, another vote was taken. This time the opposition defeated the Act of Union. Lord Castlereagh had to intensify his campaign of bribery and pressure.

The vote against the union in the Irish Parliament was soon echoed elsewhere in Ireland. Two main groups of people began to speak out against union: the barristers and a small section of leading Catholics, including Daniel O'Connell. Towards the end of 1799, a general meeting of Irish barristers was called. Fourteen senior barristers (all Protestant, by law) attended and signed a declaration that denounced the union. Some highly charged speeches were made. It was said that God made Ireland a separate kingdom, never intended her to be merely a province, and that they, the barristers, would see that she never became one.

Speaking Against the Union

Daniel O'Connell and many other younger Catholics felt that a false picture of Catholic opinion about the union had been painted by both the British government and by the Catholic leaders. They planned their own meeting to denounce the union. O'Connell organised it and made the main speech. He spoke strongly and denied that the Catholics of Ireland welcomed union with Britain. He said that the Catholics would prefer to go back to the days of the Penal Laws rather than sell their country's freedom for Catholic emancipation. To suggest otherwise was a lie.

In his first public stand, O'Connell showed his genius for avoiding trouble with the authorities and yet speaking from his heart. His speech was widely welcomed. Reported in full in the newspapers, it angered both the Catholic bishops and those rich Catholic leaders who believed in the promises of the British government.

O'Connell believed that Pitt, with his promises about emancipation, was not to be trusted. But there was steady progress towards union of the two Parliaments. During 1800, the bribery and corruption of Members of Parliament continued, and by February 1800, the government had its majority. But since the opposition still fought on, it took until the end of March to get all sections of the proposal passed.

The Act of Union came into force in January 1801. The Irish Parliament in Dublin was to be abolished; Ireland would have thirty-two members in the British House of Lords, and one hundred members in the British House of Commons.

O'Connell's first stand against the British had failed, but he was right about events after the passing of the Act. The promise of Catholic emancipation in return for supporting the union was not kept. King George III and the majority of the Cabinet overruled Pitt. A new prime minister was appointed. O'Connell was right, and the bishops and the other Catholic leaders had been wrong.

No longer in his uncle's favour because of their

disagreement about the Act of Union, the budding politician soon began work on the court circuit to earn a living. In the autumn of 1798, he took his first cases, and immediately showed his genius as a barrister, whether prosecuting or defending. Already, he was an experienced speaker who mixed humour with seriousness, and knew when to praise and when to ridicule. He soon became an expert cross-examiner. His knowledge of the country people and of the Irish language helped him greatly, and his outgoing manner inspired confidence and affection. He gained a reputation for ingenuity in getting clients acquitted, and soon crowds came to court to watch him at work.

Secret Marriage

Before long, 'Hunting Cap' decided it was time his nephew married, and he chose a bride for him – a Miss Healy from Cork. Daniel was horrified when he met her: she was very plain with an extremely long nose. But 'Hunting Cap' did not care what his nephew thought; the most important point was that this young Cork woman was a rich heiress. Having succeeded in postponing the proposed marriage, Daniel met and fell in love with a cousin of his from Tralee. Mary O'Connell was a doctor's daughter with little or no money to her name. Dan asked her to marry him, and knowing that his uncle would oppose the marriage, Mary agreed to a secret marriage in Dublin. The secret was kept for over a year, until their first child was born.

In their first year of marriage, Daniel and Mary saw little of each other. Daniel wrote her letters, addressing her as Miss O'Connell, and came down to Tralee to see her as often as he could. 'Hunting Cap' was furious, and cut Daniel out of his will altogether, leaving his estate instead to his three surviving brothers. Daniel now had to make his living from the law. His wife went to live with him in Dublin, and the young couple were gloriously happy.

The union with Britain had many effects. Because there was now no parliament in Ireland, many of the rich business people moved to London. There was no proper representation for Irish causes in the British Parliament because the Irish members seemed incapable of acting together for Ireland.

The Irish economy suffered under the union because of the long war between England and France. Ireland had to help to pay for it now. Also, more and more landlords lived in England, and the money they collected from their Irish tenants was rarely spent in Ireland. The woollen and cotton industries were unable to compete with the much larger English industries. The linen industry in Ulster was one of the few industries to benefit from the union. Englishmen with money did not invest in Ireland as they saw no prospect of making a profit; as far as they were concerned, it was a poor country, frequently disturbed and best left alone.

For the Irish who lived on small, miserable farms, this was a terrible time. They rarely saw their landlords and usually had to pay their rent to middlemen; rent continually rose and any extra money they might earn went on taxes. They knew that the middlemen who took their taxes were making money, and they resented them.

Violence became common, and small bands of secret societies developed: Whiteboys, Threshers, and Ribbonmen. All had the same purpose: to protect the tenant against the landlord. They practised terrorism and assassination.

There was a steady growth in the population. In 1800 there had been about 5,000,000 people in Ireland, but by 1821 the figure had risen to 6,800,000. It rose to 7,700,000 in 1831, and to 8,175,000 in 1841. There were no opportunities for employment in industry, and if a farmer had land and many sons, he divided it among them. This constant subdivision was commonplace, and it made living conditions worse. Most people lived on potatoes and on what they could earn from casual or seasonal work.

Daniel O'Connell saw the plight of his country and wanted to do something. He felt that the only answer was that Ireland be given back her parliament.

Hopes that the British government would grant full Catholic emancipation revived when Pitt returned to power in 1804.

Daniel O'Connell saw the plight of his country and wanted to do something

The Catholic Committee

The Catholics felt that Pitt, having promised emancipation in return for the union, would give them a sympathetic hearing. The Catholic Board – which was largely responsible for the few rights Catholics had achieved – had in 1793 been formally banned by the arm of the British government in Ireland, Dublin Castle. But a number of Catholics created a new group and gave it a new name: the Catholic Committee.

O'Connell was a prominent member of this committee, and insisted it should ask Pitt to present an emancipation bill to Parliament. The request to Pitt was signed by a hundred respected Catholics, but Pitt refused, saying that the objections of the king overruled any promises he had made. It was given to another Member of Parliament, Charles Fox. He put it before Parliament, but it was defeated by a vote of three to one. This defeat impressed on O'Connell the fact that the only hope for Catholics lay in the restoration of the Irish Parliament, as they would never be able to influence the English House of Commons.

The Catholic Committee had to move cautiously as the Catholic Board had been banned because it had claimed to represent Catholic opinion in Ireland. O'Connell told the authorities in Dublin Castle that the new Catholic Committee was not representative; it only represented itself. Through this clever use of the law, he kept the committee free from interference for a number of years.

During this period, O'Connell became known as the 'Counsellor'. He began to handle three to four court cases a day. He worked a very long day, getting up in the morning at four, working at home until eight-thirty, walking to the Four Courts at ten-thirty, spending from eleven to three there, before going to the offices of the Catholic Committee. He went home to dinner at four, sat with his family from four-thirty to six-thirty, and then worked until it was time to go to bed at ten. He spent a lot of time travelling, especially in Munster.

He and his family lived at 4 Westland Row until 1811, when they moved to 30 Merrion Square. He built up a tremendous reputation as a lawyer, and was noted for his relentless pursuit of witnesses. He had a glorious opportunity to make his views known about the union when Dublin Corporation convened a special meeting of the freemen and freeholders of the city. The objective was to support a resolution passed by the corporation condemning the closing of the Irish Parliament. O'Connell made a long, detailed speech about what had happened to Ireland as a result of the union whilst condemning the British government's policy of attempting to make two kinds of Irishmen: Protestant and Catholic. He said: 'They falsely declared that we hated each other, and they continued to repeat this assertion until we came to believe it.'

Dublin Castle was shocked by O'Connell's speech, and began to watch the Catholic Committee, determined to trap them into doing something illegal. The committee had regular monthly meetings, and one of these was interrupted by a representative of Dublin Castle, who asked them to disperse. On being asked by O'Connell and other barristers the legal basis for this request, he left.

Some months later, a magistrate called Mr Hare came and asked the chairman the reason for the meeting. Mr Hare tried to get the chairman to say that the people attending the meeting had been chosen (which would have made the meeting illegal), but the chairman, Lord Fingal, said they were at the meeting solely to petition Parliament. The magistrate said that answer would not do, and if Lord Fingal refused to answer his question, the magistrate would take his refusal as a confession of guilt. Lord Fingal did not answer, and Mr Hare ordered the people at the meeting to disperse. When the chairman refused to leave his chair, Mr Hare arrested him. A number of other people took the chair, and they were arrested. The meeting broke up, but when those who were arrested asked the police about bail, they were told they could go free. Dublin Castle's clumsy attempts to silence the Catholic Committee sparked protest meetings all round the country – their plans had backfired.

The Catholic Committee was more hopeful about emancipation when George III was forced to retire, and the Prince of Wales took his place as regent. The prince had been friendly to the Catholic cause, but hopes were short-lived because, on assuming power, he showed that he had changed his mind. The Catholic Committee met in Dublin and spelled out its sense of disappointment. Speaking at the meeting, O'Connell detailed at least four occasions when the prince had promised that when he became king he would give the Catholics their full rights.

O'Connell was at the height of his power. He could sway multitudes with a whisper, a small gesture, or a movement of his expressive face. His humour – absent only from his most serious speeches – gave him unrivalled power over crowds.

A new challenger to O'Connell was appointed. Robert Peel was only twenty-four when he arrived in Dublin as Irish secretary, and he was shocked to learn of the methods of government practised in Ireland. He wrote to the prime minister, Lord Liverpool, explaining that he saw very little hope of reforming the Irish system of administration so that it would resemble the British system. Lord Liverpool said that he must continue governing in Ireland even if he had to buy support.

> **… he must continue governing in Ireland even if he had to buy support**

In the meantime, O'Connell had been touring the country addressing meetings. He was determined to rouse the people. When he heard of the arrival of the new Irish secretary, and though he knew very little about him, he called him a 'raw youth' who had been sent over 'before he got over the foppery of perfumed handkerchiefs and thin shoes.'

O'Connell's speeches were widely reported, and Peel was intensely annoyed.

The Evening Post

Since the abolition of the Irish Parliament in 1801, Dublin Castle had been the centre of British rule in Ireland (and remained so until 1922). Power in Ireland rested in the hands of the viceroy, two undersecretaries, the attorney general, and the chief secretary.

When Robert Peel was appointed chief secretary, he saw that his new position did not give him enough power. But he waited and noted how much influence a previous chief secretary, Lord Castlereagh, had had just before the union. His opportunity came with the resignation of the Duke of Richmond as viceroy within a year of his arrival in Dublin, and by the resignation, at the same time, of one of the viceroy's undersecretaries.

Peel was now the most powerful man in Ireland and with the help of the attorney general, William Saurin, decided to quell the Catholic agitation for emancipation. However, several members of the British cabinet who saw the need for Catholic emancipation – and openly promoted it – hampered Peel.

When the House of Commons met, the Catholics had high hopes that emancipation would be granted. Since 1808, Henry Grattan had been petitioning for Catholic emancipation before the British Houses of Parliament. However, he knew that a principal reason that Protestants resisted emancipation was their fear that the allegiance of Catholics to the pope would keep them from being good subjects of the English crown. The Irish bishops had met in secret and agreed that if emancipation were granted, they would allow the British government to have a veto on the appointment of Catholic bishops whom the British thought politically dangerous. Knowing of this meeting, Henry Grattan proposed the idea to the British Parliament. He thought it perfectly reasonable, but when the majority of the Catholics heard of the proposed veto, it was condemned out of hand. They felt it would be interference by the state into church affairs.

Only the rich Catholics supported the proposal. O'Connell and the Catholic Committee vigorously opposed it. Soon the hierarchy was frightened into rejecting it. But Grattan proceeded with his motion to the House of Commons. The first year it was defeated in the Commons by 281 votes to 128. Every year thereafter Grattan introduced it and the opposition in the House of Commons gradually decreased. Soon, Catholic emancipation was actually passed in the House of Commons, but opposition by the House of Lords continued until it was forced to change in 1829.

Two British members of the House of Lords proposed a further compromise that they felt would please everybody. A commission would be set up in England and Ireland to approve appointments of bishops; it would consist mainly of landowners. This new proposal further divided the various organisations campaigning for emancipation. The English Catholic Board (a body resembling O'Connell's Catholic Committee) was delighted. The English hierarchy rejected the idea totally. In Ireland, both the hierarchy and the Catholic Committee rejected it. Grattan, however, thought that the new proposal was an excellent one and brought it before the House of Commons, but it was defeated.

O'Connell was pleased with the defeat of Grattan's bill, as it would not have had the support of Irish Catholics. He felt that Grattan was no longer the man to promote the Catholic cause, and at a meeting of the Catholic Committee, he attacked the idea that the crown needed a veto before giving the Catholics freedom. He emphasised the affection of the Irish people for the British crown, and pointed out how many Irishmen had given their lives for Britain in wars.

Whenever O'Connell spoke, he had to emphasise his own allegiance and that of his followers to the British crown. It was rumoured that he and the Catholic Committee were seeking to make Ireland a separate country from England. Again and again, he insisted that he sought a separate parliament for Ireland because it would serve Ireland better, but never wished to be separate from the king.

... he sought a separate parliament for Ireland ...

Everywhere he went, the people greeted him with tremendous warmth. He felt he could easily organise the people to support his attempt to get Catholic emancipation and restoration of the Irish Parliament.

Meanwhile, Dublin Castle was watching every move he made, and was eager to trap him or any member of the Catholic Committee. O'Connell continued to attack methods of government in Ireland. He drew attention to attacks on Catholics by Orange lodges in Ulster and in Dublin. He condemned Dublin Castle's new methods of ensuring that they obtained the 'right' verdicts in court cases – appointing all-Protestant juries. His education in France and in London, and his experience at the Irish Bar, had prepared him well for his life's work. He was making highly emotional speeches, like this one:

> *I could not be an Irishman if I did not feel grateful at the way you received me today. Sorry, sunk and degraded as my country is, I still glory in the title of Irishman. Those humble efforts I have put into trying to achieve freedom for my country have been a delightful duty for me. I swear here and now that my life is at her service.*

In 1813 on the retirement of the viceroy, the Duke of Richmond, *the Evening Post* ran a series of articles describing the administration of the country under him and his predecessors:

> *They insulted, they oppressed, they murdered, and they deceived. The profligate and unprincipled Westmoreland, the coldhearted and cruel Camden, the artful and treacherous Cornwallis left Ireland more depressed and divided than they had found her.*

The owner of the *Evening Post* was a Protestant, John Magee. He had devoted the *Evening Post* almost completely to covering the progress of the Catholic Committee. He felt it would help sales. Dublin Castle had been waiting for an opportunity to take action. Through a libel case that they now brought against John Magee, they wanted to cause a division between Catholics and those Protestants who supported the Catholic Committee.

O'Connell, however, defended Magee in court, and was too shrewd for them. He anticipated their every move, and managed to turn the libel action against Magee into an opportunity to promote the views of the Catholic Committee and to indict the rule of Dublin Castle.

The trial began in early July 1813. On the opening day, William Saurin, the attorney general, used such language as this: 'My Lords, you will be shocked to hear that the defendant is indicted with charging His Grace the Duke of Richmond with being a murderer.' O'Connell opposed every move Saurin made, showing that the attorney general had made inaccurate statements, and accusing him of pronouncing Magee guilty before the trial had even properly begun.

O'Connell managed to get a postponement of the

trial until 26 July. When it reopened, everything was stacked against Magee. Dublin Castle had ensured that the twelve-man jury was Protestant and that none of them supported the Catholic cause.

O'Connell allowed Saurin the freedom of the first day to state his case, but on the second day, he stood up to begin a marathon four-hour speech. He began with a hopeless appeal to the jury to have an open mind. Next, he attacked the speech made by the attorney general, and described it as containing neither order, method nor eloquence. He accused Saurin of descending to the language of the streets and of calling John Magee foul names. He wondered how Mr Saurin had learned such names since he was for so many years used to the language of polished society.

O'Connell then told the jury that he did not like to bring politics into the case, but already the attorney general had. Mr Saurin, he said, had stated that Catholics in Ireland had been learning principles of a seditious, treasonable and revolutionary nature. Mr Saurin had accused the members of the Catholic Board of all these things.

> *But if any man dares charge the Catholic Committee or any individual of the committee with sedition or treason, I shall*

always, anywhere this happens, brand him as an infamous and profligate liar.

O'Connell went on to state exactly what the Catholic Committee had always been looking for – the rights of Catholics under the constitution. Mr Saurin was wrong to boast that he would eventually put down the Catholic Committee, for it was a lawful body. He repeated the rights of Catholics to look for freedom:

The sons of even distinguished earls cannot in their native land attain honourable positions yet these same positions are open to every son of a bigoted and intemperate stranger who might decide to come to Ireland.

He raised his voice until it thundered in the courtroom as it did at monster public meetings:

This system cannot last; he may insult, he may calumniate, he may prosecute but the Catholic cause is on the march; its progress is rapid and obvious, its success is just as certain as the return of tomorrow's eve.

Turning to the jury, O'Connell appealed to them not to disgrace their honour and religion by agreeing to the attorney general's prosecution. He read out the article in the *Evening Post*, justified it sentence by sentence, gave the jury a lecture on the importance of freedom of the press, and read extracts from speeches made by Saurin when Saurin was a barrister. In those speeches, he had been totally opposed to the union with Britain. He had become attorney general as a reward for changing his mind. The point was not lost on the jury and the packed courtroom. Finally, O'Connell read extracts from a newspaper that supported the government. There were sentences encouraging Orangemen to avenge themselves for murders that had never taken place.

'Was that paper prosecuted?' he asked the jury. He provided the answer himself:

On the contrary the paper is paid large sums of public money. There are no less than five examples in this paper of this kind of exhortation to Orangemen and yet despite these obvious libels the two proprietors of this newspaper have each a pension of £400 per annum; for supporting the government, it is called. Since the time of the publication of this edition one of the proprietors has got a government job worth £800 per year while the son of the other has been given a job worth £400.

Although the verdict against Magee was inevitable, O'Connell's speech roused Catholic feeling in Ireland more than any other speech he had made. Here, a Catholic lawyer, faced with all the powers of Dublin Castle and opposed by the attorney general himself, had spoken out as a proud Irishman and condemned the system of government. By his skilful use of the trial, O'Connell had done a tremendous job for Catholic emancipation. His speech was fully reported in the newspapers and then printed in pamphlet form. After Magee was convicted, O'Connell entered an appeal. When the case came before the court again, Saurin maintained that Magee deserved more punishment for publishing the full speech made by O'Connell in the court. He also attacked O'Connell directly, accusing him of trying to frighten him from doing his duty as a public servant. Saurin considered 'that such an outrage on public decency had not occurred in the history of man.'

O'Connell replied by saying that if the attorney general had made such an attack anywhere else, he would have given him a beating. There was consternation in court, but after much legal argument there was a withdrawal by both men. The court gave a clear verdict against Magee, and he was sentenced to two years' imprisonment with fines of up to £500. The success of this prosecution showed that any Protestant who publicly helped the Catholic cause would be in trouble.

The Duel

During this period, O'Connell attacked Dublin Corporation in one of his public speeches. Although the corporation had been against the union with Britain in 1800, under pressure from Dublin Castle, it now supported it. O'Connell accused the corporation of being 'beggarly' in its approach.

A member of the corporation, named D'Esterre, resented O'Connell's speech. D'Esterre had backed the Catholic cause, but now was in financial trouble. He decided to seek election as a sheriff, but his support of the Catholics jeopardised his chances of being elected. He wrote a rude letter to O'Connell in which he demanded to know if he had in fact said what he was reported to have said in the newspapers; if so, he requested a reply that same evening.

O'Connell was aware that D'Esterre was the only alderman to vote for the Catholics, but he felt that a rude letter demanded an equally rude reply. He repeated in even stronger terms what he had said about the corporation. This angered D'Esterre, and knowing that O'Connell objected to duelling, he decided to provoke him, believing that O'Connell would refuse and thus be disgraced.

One day, D'Esterre waited outside the Four Courts with a horsewhip in his hand. He was a small man, and a crowd gathered to see the fun as the small figure attempted to whip the large frame of O'Connell. O'Connell was forced by a judge to avoid a confrontation with D'Esterre that day, but the quarrel continued.

O'Connell knew that a duel was inevitable. He appointed a 'second' (an assistant at a duel), and borrowed duelling pistols from his friend Richard Bennet. On 1 February 1815 another member of Dublin Corporation approached Major MacNamara, O'Connell's second, and said that if O'Connell apologised, D'Esterre would withdraw. Major MacNamara replied that the duel was to be held that evening at Bishops Court Field, just outside Naas.

O'Connell arrived at the field with his old friend Bennet, his brother James, two seconds, and Macklin his surgeon. The duel was to be held on a slope screened by trees on all sides and hidden from the road by a high wall. There was a thin layer of snow on the ground.

D'Esterre was late, and news of the duel spread. From all the surrounding countryside, people came. D'Esterre finally arrived, accompanied by his brother, nearly all the members of Dublin Corporation, and some officials of the government. All were well armed to protect themselves in the event of O'Connell being killed.

While waiting, O'Connell prayed. The Church forbade Catholics to duel, but a friend of the family, Father Mullane, waited in a hut nearby in case he would be needed.

At last it was time, and O'Connell's second, Major MacNamara, won the toss for position, and the two men advanced within ten paces of each other. A handkerchief was raised. When it dropped, the two men fired. D'Esterre's shot hit the ground beside O'Connell, but O'Connell's hit D'Esterre in the hip. He bled profusely, staining the snow.

The surgeon examined him and said that he would be all right. There was great rejoicing that no life had been lost. O'Connell returned at once with his friends to his family at Merrion Square. Soon the people heard the news and bonfires were lit all around Dublin. 'O'Connell is safe,' the people cried.

The next morning, however, news came that D'Esterre's wound was not healing. He admitted that he had provoked O'Connell and that the responsibility for his death would be his own. He died two days later.

O'Connell was shocked, and regarded himself as a murderer. He wrote to D'Esterre's widow, offering to share his income with her and her two children. She declined his offer, but asked him to support her small daughter. O'Connell did this for the rest of his life.

The memory of the duel always haunted him. He never went to Holy Communion afterwards without wearing a glove on his right hand as a sign of penance, and whenever he passed D'Esterre's house on Bachelor's Walk, he would raise his hat and utter a silent prayer for him.

Despite his regret, he would shortly get into a quarrel that almost led to a duel with the chief secretary, Robert Peel.

Sir Robert Peel

The chances that Catholics would get their full rights from the British government all but vanished with the defeat of Napoleon in 1814. When the war with France was over, England no longer needed Catholics to join its army, and felt it no longer needed to grant Catholic rights. This was shown clearly when Robert Peel banned the Catholic Board.

Peel was bitterly disappointed that D'Esterre had failed to kill O'Connell, and he waited for an opportunity to do the job himself. While O'Connell continued his career as a barrister, Peel continued his campaign to outwit him.

O'Connell, in despair about the future of Irish Catholics and their rights, began to make bitter speeches. Hearing that Peel had made a speech against him in the House of Commons, he decided to attack

Peel at a public meeting. However, his information was incorrect: Peel had merely said that O'Connell was a formidable opponent – but O'Connell repeated his public attack. He accused Peel of being afraid to confront him in person. It was the opportunity for which Peel had been waiting. He immediately sent a friend of his – an official from Dublin Castle named Sir Charles Saxton – to demand an explanation from O'Connell. O'Connell refused to give one, and said he would stand by anything he had said in public concerning the chief secretary.

O'Connell then sent his friend George Lidwell to see Peel. Lidwell discovered that O'Connell's information had been incorrect, and reported this to him. A few days later, an account of the whole incident appeared in a local newspaper, *The Correspondent*. It had been sent in by Saxton, and contained an obvious sneer at O'Connell for shirking a duel.

O'Connell answered by printing his side of the story in another newspaper, the *Carrick Post*. This made Peel even angrier, and he sent a challenge to O'Connell. Alarmed, Mrs O'Connell sent for the sheriff and had her husband arrested for proposing to take part in a duel. At the same time, Lidwell – O'Connell's second – was also arrested, the sheriff having been sent for by his daughter. The two appeared in court the next day, and they were bound by the judge to keep the peace and to a bond of £10,000.

Knowing that he could never duel in Ireland, O'Connell sent word to Peel that they should meet in France. Peel and Saxton went openly to France; their departure and purpose were announced in the newspapers. O'Connell eluded his wife and went to England, but the British government was waiting for him. The idea was to arrest him and insult him by not allowing him to fight the duel. Lidwell and O'Connell nevertheless reached London, but they were delayed there whilst awaiting a passport. They avoided the police by changing their lodgings a few times, but the police finally caught up with them as they were about to step into the coach for Dover.

The court told them that if they held the duel, the survivor would be tried for murder, and so after a month in London, O'Connell set out for home. It was his last involvement in a duel.

The period between 1815 and 1823 was a depressing one for O'Connell and a terrible one for Ireland. The potato blight struck in 1817. The leaves of the plants curled, the potatoes rotted, and there was a stench in the fields. Famine followed.

Despite this, O'Connell continued to try to rouse his people. Each year, he asked his countrymen for 'one last effort'. But the public was not listening. In a way, the people had given up hope.

He went on with his court work and was earning the large sum of £8,000 a year, but he had to work very hard. We can get see how difficult it was for O'Connell from a letter written to him by his wife:

My dearest love,

I wish to God you would continue to get out of court for a quarter of an hour during the middle of the day to take a bowl of soup or a snack of some kind. Surely, though you may not be able to spare time to go to a tavern, could not James get anything you wished from the bar mess at your lodgings, which is merely a step from the court house. Do, my Heart, try to accomplish this; for I am quite unhappy to have you fasting from an early hour in the morning until nine or ten at night. I wish I was with you to make you take care of yourself.

Your loving wife, Mary.

The Reawakening of the Irish Nation

O'Connell kept hoping that he could reawaken the Irish nation. He campaigned through letters to the papers and speeches, but nothing seemed to work. The year 1819 passed. Then 1820, 1821, 1822 – and still no sign of awakening. There was a slight change in Dublin Castle in 1822, when a new viceroy – an Irishman, Lord Wellesley – ousted his old enemy, William Saurin, who, after Peel's departure in 1818, had become the main power in Dublin Castle.

That same year, at a meeting with some old friends, O'Connell first put forward plans for a new form of agitation. He wanted to involve all the people of Ireland in an enormous movement to force the government to give Catholics their rights. O'Connell and Richard Shiel were determined to act, and it took them a full year to organise a meeting of prominent Catholics. At this meeting in May 1823 O'Connell proposed the founding of a Catholic Association. It was to be much more open than either the Catholic Board or the Catholic Committee. Anyone could join on paying an annual subscription of one guinea. There was one exception – Catholic priests throughout the country were automatically made honorary members.

O'Connell received some forty-six subscriptions immediately, but the idea did not grow until a year later when he made a new proposal: any person could become an associate member of the Catholic Association by paying one shilling a year. This could be paid by the people at the church doors at the rate of a penny a month. When O'Connell's motion was passed, the collecting of this 'Catholic Rent' began.

Many of his enemies laughed at his new idea, but they were not pleased when they saw it succeed. In a few months, £100 a week was collected; by December 1824, £700 a week; by 1825, at least £1,000 a week. The association was also helped by one of Ireland's youngest bishops – Dr Doyle, bishop of Kildare and Leighlin – who joined as a full member.

The money available allowed O'Connell to found a newspaper, the *Morning Register*, which published full reports of the association's activities. Money was also used to pay lawyers to defend members of the association brought to court for not paying tithes.

With his practice at the bar, O'Connell now had almost no leisure time. But when travelling about the country attending court, he noticed his increasing popularity. People gathered to watch him in court and kept him up all night talking. They were not dismayed by his losing cases for some of his Catholic clients. They saw that he could not possibly sway carefully chosen juries. They believed in him. He was their 'Liberator', and he would rescue them.

The increasing influence of the Catholic Association was watched with alarm in Westminster. Robert Peel, now home secretary, hoped that O'Connell would make a slip so that he could be put in jail. He felt that the only way to stop the Catholic Association was to stop O'Connell, and his opportunity came in December 1825 when O'Connell made a speech praising the South American struggle for liberty. Dublin Castle was ordered to bring a charge against O'Connell.

The case came before the court the following year, and it failed miserably. None of the newspaper reporters would say what they had heard at the meeting of the Catholic Association, where the speech was made. The stupidity of the government in bringing this flimsy case against O'Connell was shown up. O'Connell made full use of it at the next meeting of the association, emphasising that the association wanted Irishmen to have rights equal to those enjoyed by Englishmen.

... Dublin Castle was ordered to bring a charge against O'Connell

Peel was defeated, but with the support of the king – who felt that the association was threatening rebellion – he decided to bring a new bill into Parliament: a Bill for the Suppression of Unlawful Associations in Ireland. This was to be debated before the House of Commons in February.

When Dan's old uncle 'Hunting Cap' died in Derrynane at the age of ninety-seven, Daniel was unable to attend the funeral because he had to go to London to try to stop Peel's bill. He was amazed at the reaction of the English to his presence. People stood in the street to see him pass in his coach, and he was asked to speak at many meetings. He was brought to the House of Commons by British Members of Parliament to meet and talk to members opposed to the Catholic cause.

The House of Lords held an inquiry into the state of Ireland, and both Daniel and Bishop Doyle were to give evidence. O'Connell explained the true position of the Catholic Association, and his approach was having an affect. He met members of the English Association, and impressed them.

Because of his meetings in London and his work in Ireland, a bill for Catholic emancipation was again to be brought before the House of Commons. O'Connell was asked to prepare it himself.

Daniel was hopeful – so much so that he was willing to see the Catholic Association disbanded as a gesture of goodwill. He met the Duke of York and received a very kind welcome from him. But he was being deceived. When the bill had been passed by the House of Commons, it came before the House of Lords, where it was defeated due to violent opposition from the same Duke of York.

O'Connell was bitterly disappointed. He went home, disillusioned once again with British justice. After the Catholic emancipation bill was rejected, a bill to suppress the Catholic Association was drawn up and passed. But there was a loophole in the new law: it did not prohibit societies that existed for purely charitable purposes. Immediately, O'Connell set up the New Catholic Association, an organisation 'for the relief of distressed Catholics'. This new organisation began its regular monthly meetings in July 1825, and became responsible for the collection of the Catholic Rent.

O'Connell was not beaten, and he began to see new results in his long fight. His popularity grew every month. He had a flair for extraordinary clothes and always wore a huge cape, a blue coat, a yellow waistcoat, white trousers, a black velvet collar, and a gilt collar-button. He was showing off, but the people loved him, and where he went they followed, often carrying him shoulder-high through towns and villages. But the growth of the association had another important effect: all around the country, new leaders, with their own ideas, were appearing.

O'Connell began a new campaign to stir up the people. Different parts of the country began to compete to see who could have the largest crowds. The organisation and effort the various groups put into the meetings was greater than anything that had gone before. The new leaders of the association around the country began to think up schemes of their own.

It was just such a scheme that put O'Connell on the road to victory. Thomas Wyse in Waterford suggested that the association should put forward a candidate to contest the 1826 general election in Waterford City. He chose a young Protestant landlord called Villiers Stuart to stand as their candidate. O'Connell felt there was no hope of success, and thought that the forty-shilling freeholders would never vote against their landlords, the mighty Beresfords.

The landlords were furious. Lord George Beresford and the other landlords warned their tenants not to vote for Villiers Stuart. But even Thomas Wyse was amazed at the reaction of the voters all round Waterford. Many meetings were held, and crowds of Catholics held green branches as a symbol of the revolt. When O'Connell heard this, he hurried down to help the campaign. He was greeted with overwhelming enthusiasm everywhere he went.

The Election

This election was a model for future campaigns by the association. The butchers in the town formed themselves into a civic guard and patrolled the streets controlling the crowds. The defeat of the Beresfords was massive. Villiers Stuart was voted in by the poor people, who O'Connell had thought would not have the courage to vote against their landlords.

It was too late to organise wide-scale election contests in many other areas, but association candidates did stand in Louth, Monaghan and Westmeath, and they won. The reaction of the landlords was to be expected. Wholesale evictions of tenants followed.

There was still no sign that the government would give in to Catholic emancipation. But O'Connell was certain that if he showed that the people of Ireland were now speaking with one voice, the British would not be able to resist. Meanwhile, he tried to help evicted tenants by raising a special rent through the association.

The Duke of Wellington became prime minister in January 1828. Because of the change of government, an election was held in Co. Clare. Vesey Fitzgerald stood, and the result seemed a foregone conclusion, as Fitzgerald was a popular landlord and a supporter of the cause of Catholic emancipation.

However, the Catholic Association saw the election as an opportunity to demonstrate its power. Members of the association in Dublin decided that O'Connell himself should stand. He tried to refuse, saying that he could not afford the expense. The man who had asked him to stand was not upset – he asked for subscriptions for O'Connell in the papers the following morning. In ten days, £28,000 had been collected for the campaign.

Immediately, O'Connell attacked the system by which Catholics were refused entry into Parliament:

It is true that as a Catholic I cannot and never will take the oaths at present prescribed to Members of Parliament but the authority which created these oaths can cancel them; and I entertain a confident hope that if you elect me, even the most unreasonable of your enemies will see the necessity of removing from the chosen representative of the people an obstacle which would prevent him from doing his duty to his king and his country.

O'Connell went on to show just how distasteful the oaths were to Catholics.

It was some days before O'Connell could leave Dublin, but when he did, cheering crowds surrounded his carriage. His old friend Richard Bennet accompanied him. The journey down to Clare was like the procession of a king. At Roscrea – where they stopped to attend Mass – huge crowds gathered to welcome them; at Nenagh, their coach was escorted by 3,000 mounted men; at Limerick, they were met by a procession of people from all the trades in the city; in Clare, there was a bonfire on every hill. An exhausted O'Connell retired to bed for a few hours' rest.

The following morning, the nomination of candidates took place in Ennis, and then the campaign began in earnest. O'Connell used all his powers of oration to win over the people, making it clear that his victory would force the British government to grant Catholics rights.

The election was well organised. Temporary shelters had been built in Ennis to accommodate the huge crowds that came in from remote villages. Kitchens were set up to feed them. There was strict supervision of the crowds to ensure that there would be neither drinking nor fighting.

The result was easily foreseen: O'Connell won by a two-to-one majority. It was more than just an election victory. It was a victory for the cause of Catholic emancipation.

... victory for the cause ...

The following spring, the prime minister sent Robert Peel into the House of Commons to see that the Catholic emancipation bill was passed. The prime minister himself undertook to bring the bill through the House of Lords on 5 March 1829. It had been a long, hard struggle, but it was only the beginning of O'Connell's fight to get justice and liberty for his fellow Irishmen.

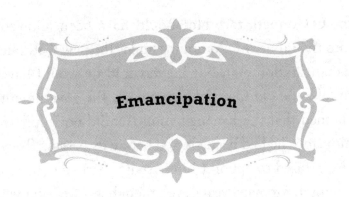

Emancipation

The Catholic Emancipation Act was passed in March 1829 because of mass agitation by the people of Ireland, and it was a marvellous victory for O'Connell.

Catholics were now eligible for government jobs in all countries under British rule. Catholics could also enter Parliament, since they were obliged only to take an oath denying the supremacy of the pope over civil matters.

But at the same time, the British Parliament suppressed organisations like the Catholic Association through the Act for the Suppression of Illegal Associations. They also directly attacked the people who voted for O'Connell and other Members of Parliament in favour of emancipation by removing the vote from forty-shilling freeholders, thereby reducing the voting population of Ireland from 200,000 to 26,000.

The British government tried to make life difficult

for O'Connell, too. He should have been allowed into the House of Commons under the new Catholic Emancipation Act, but he was told he would have to take the old Oath of Supremacy. The government claimed that the Emancipation Act did not apply to him since he had been elected before its passing. They also refused to appoint him a senior barrister (King's Counsel) for many years, even though less well-known lawyers achieved that status. Though O'Connell was fifty years old, he still had to earn a living as a junior barrister, taking every case that came along, even if it was worth only a few guineas.

O'Connell decided to try to take his seat in Parliament. He came into the House of Commons on 15 May 1829. He was handed printed copies of the oaths he was expected to take before he could take his seat. One of these was the Oath of Supremacy, and the other was against the Mass and adoration of the Virgin Mary and other saints. O'Connell read them out to the House word for word, said he would never accept them, and walked out.

A Second Election

O'Connell had to stand for his seat in Parliament again and so the Catholic Association provided money for him to do so. In this election, O'Connell focused on what he regarded as the only solution to the problems of Ireland – repeal of the Act of Union. During the thirty years since the union, the country's industries had declined, trade in the towns had gone down considerably, and there had been a series of repressive laws.

Everywhere he went for his election campaign, O'Connell was welcomed by huge crowds who showed they appreciated what he had done for them. They wanted to be represented in Parliament by a Catholic leader who would speak for them. Clare re-elected O'Connell without opposition on 30 July 1829.

Knowing that he must soon concentrate on his career in the British Parliament, he decided to go for a long rest to Derrynane and refused to take any court cases that summer. While O'Connell was in Derrynane, an extraordinary murder case came before the courts in Cork. An attempt had been made to murder an unpopular magistrate in Doneraile, and the crown, acting on a tip from informers, brought a charge against some local farmers and labourers. Solicitor general Doherty was prosecuting for Dublin Castle. On the first day of the trial and with a hand-picked jury, he obtained a conviction against four of the men, and they were condemned to death. They were to be hanged within six days. This was on a Saturday; the rest of the men were to appear in court on the following Monday.

The defence lawyers felt that the only one who could save these men was O'Connell, and a messenger set out on horseback to Derrynane. He rode all Saturday night and through Sunday morning. O'Connell first saw the tired messenger coming down the mountain road. He assured O'Connell immediately that every one of the men was innocent, and told him that Doherty would have all the men hanged if he did not come.

O'Connell immediately sent a messenger to Cork to tell the defence lawyers he was on his way. He then set off in a horse and carriage.

The court case began promptly at nine o'clock

on the Monday morning. The defence solicitor was refused a postponement, so the case was progressing when O'Connell burst into the courtroom wearing neither wig nor gown. He apologised to the judges and asked if a bowl of milk and some sandwiches might be brought into the court. This request was granted, and so O'Connell sat down to listen to Doherty's case.

He began to challenge him on every point of law. Many times during Doherty's address to the jury, O'Connell made objections. Then O'Connell turned his attention to the three informers. He bullied them until they did not know what they were saying or what they had said. By the afternoon, he had confessions from the informers which contradicted the evidence they had already given. He also made nonsense of the evidence given by the other witnesses for the prosecution. He directly attacked the solicitor general, scorning his grasp of the law and mimicking his genteel accent. By the end of the day, it was clear that even a hand-picked jury could not convict the men.

The jury left the court to consider its verdict. Though they argued for a full day and a half, they failed to come to a decision, and the judge discharged them. Another jury was appointed, and the case began again. In relentless cross-examination, O'Connell persuaded one of the informers to admit swearing to two different versions of the story. It was inevitable that a verdict of not guilty would be returned, and even the death sentence on the first four men was commuted.

O'Connell was loved all the more by the people. But he was in financial trouble. He had to go to London and take his seat in Parliament. This meant having three houses – one each in London, Dublin and Derrynane – and his only means of making a living was to work as a junior barrister. At that time, Members of Parliament were not paid. (If they voted with the government, they received gifts, bribes and government jobs for themselves and their relations.) O'Connell still hoped to become a senior barrister, but King George IV was against making him the first Catholic senior barrister. When the government insisted that the king appoint some Catholic senior barristers, the secretary of the English Catholic Board, Charles Butler – now eighty years old – was appointed, along with some Irishmen, including a friend of O'Connell's, Richard Shiel.

P.V. Fitzpatrick – the Dublin merchant who had organised the subscription for O'Connell's election in Clare – came up with the solution to his financial problem. He would organise a collection as a tribute to O'Connell throughout Ireland. Fitzpatrick collected £30,000 in the first year. Though worried at first about taking the money, O'Connell eventually gave up his career as a barrister and was very dependent on the tribute. He felt that the Irish people were paying him to work for them in Parliament.

The tribute averaged about £13,000 a year. He spoke this way of it himself:

> *But I dreamed a day-dream or was it a dream? That Ireland still wanted me; that although the Catholic aristocracy had obtained most valuable advantages from Catholic Emancipation, yet the benefit of good government had not reached the great mass of the Irish people and could not reach them unless the Union be abolished.*

He spoke at public meetings about what he would like to achieve in Parliament. He wanted every man over twenty-one to be given the vote. He wanted voting to be by secret ballot. He wanted the union rejected. But his experience in the House of Commons was depressing. As a private member, he could get very little done. The Tories – among them Wellington and Peel – were in power, and they prevented him from achieving much as they hated him because he had forced them to grant Catholic emancipation.

O'Connell decided to form an organisation in Ireland to campaign for repeal of the Act of Union. It was to be called the 'Anti-Union Association', and the newspapers carried notices from O'Connell proclaiming a public meeting of the new organisation. But he did not realise that much greater powers had been given to the government by the new Act for the Suppression of Illegal Associations. The chief secretary, Sir Henry Hardinge, immediately banned the new organisation. O'Connell openly insulted the chief secretary, calling him a paltry, contemptible, little English soldier. Sir Henry immediately sent O'Connell a challenge, which O'Connell ignored. He set up another organisation under another name, but it was also suppressed. Then he announced that he would hold special breakfasts in a hotel, and outwitted the authorities as they could not think of a way to ban these.

O'Connell knew that he could not achieve much until the Tory government was beaten and the Whigs came to power. In 1839 he helped to bring down the Tories with his vote in the House of Commons, and was full of hope for the future of Ireland.

The first thing the Whigs did was to try to buy him off by offering him the job of master of the rolls or, if he did not want that, the job of attorney general. These were two of the highest positions in the Irish legal world, but O'Connell turned them down and kept his independence. When he returned to Dublin from London, he was welcomed by a huge crowd outside his home in Merrion Square. They knew that he had been offered a job:

> *They wanted me to join them ... they asked me what I wished to have done for myself. Like a true Irishman I answered their question, I answered them by asking them another. 'Tell me,' said I, 'what are you going to do for Ireland?'*

There was a cheer from the huge crowd.

> *I told you, that if you took my advice, we would achieve Emancipation. Did I deceive you? Let me tell you now if you take my advice we will repeal the Union.*

He talked, too, about his desire to achieve freedom without shedding blood:

> *France waded through blood to liberty, the Poles are wading through blood, but mark my words my friends, the shedding of one drop of blood in Ireland would effectively destroy all chance of repealing the Union. Ireland will be quiet, Ireland will be tranquil and we shall obtain our freedom by uniting among ourselves.*

Now that the Whigs were in power, O'Connell decided to go further in his campaign for repeal, and formed a repeal organisation. It was repeatedly banned by Dublin Castle. Over the next few months, O'Connell invented many names for his organisation, and all were banned.

The Castle soon decided to arrest O'Connell. The policemen who came to arrest him asked him as a favour to travel to the police station in a covered carriage. He refused, and walked to the station under police escort with most of Dublin looking on. When he appeared in court under the Act for the Suppression of Illegal Associations, he said he would plead guilty in return for a postponement of the trial. The attorney general agreed to this, and the case was deferred until late April. Meanwhile, the Whig government needed his vote in the House of Commons, and he went to London. The Whigs insisted on his staying in London, and they would not allow him to return to Dublin for his trial. Finally, when Parliament was dissolved in May, the Act under which he had been arrested lapsed, and so the case against him was dropped. He was a free man once again.

Now O'Connell's hopes were pinned on what had brought about the dissolution of Parliament – a bill for the reform of Parliament. It seemed to him that under this law, he would have much more power. Ireland, with its large and increasing population, would have many more members in the House of Commons – members who, like him, were repealers.

But when the Reform Parliament Bill was passed, it was a bitter disappointment. He had asked the government to restore the vote to forty-shilling freeholders in rural areas, but instead of doing so, they had taken it from the forty-shilling freeholders in the towns. Nevertheless, in the election, Ireland returned forty-five Members of Parliament (out of 105) who were repealers. O'Connell was determined to see what he could achieve by working solely through Parliament. He tried allying himself with the Whig government, supporting them in their general policy in the hope of securing some rights for Ireland. He did not organise much public agitation, though he did support the growing campaign to abolish the paying of tithes by tenant farmers.

The tithes – first introduced as part of the Penal Laws – provided financial support to the Protestant clergy. Even Catholics paid them, and they were always a cause of resentment. Now, in the early 1830s, a bloody campaign started to abolish them. The societies that had long been active against landlords began to concentrate on a campaign against tithes. There was much disturbance in country areas: in 1832, for example, there were 242 murders, 300 attempted murders, and hundreds of attacks on persons and property.

The British answer to the outcry against tithes was another law to suppress the violence. It was six years before the British government did anything about the tithes themselves. At last, they introduced a scheme whereby the tithes would be included in each tenant's rent, and the landlord would then be responsible for paying the money. O'Connell's long fight against tithes in Parliament had succeeded.

His unofficial cooperation with the Whig government did have some other effects. He was able to have some say about appointments to legal positions in Ireland; for example, O'Loghlen – a Catholic barrister – was appointed solicitor general.

But much was going wrong for O'Connell at this time. He was constantly attacked both in London and at home. His opponents took him to court charging him with improper practices in the 1835 election. The resulting court case cost him a lot of money. He was finding it more difficult to live on the tribute, which was decreasing because the people did not understand why their Liberator was cooperating so openly with a British government. He longed for the peace and quiet of Derrynane, but could rarely go there. Just as he was under so much pressure from every side, his wife Mary died in September 1837. He was heartbroken:

> *The man who is happiest in his family circle, may have some idea of my happiness when I was her husband. Did I say was? Oh – yes, I am her husband still. The grave may separate us for a time, but we shall meet beyond it, never I trust to be separated more.*

Soon, he became more hopeful for the future of Ireland. A young queen took the throne, and a new under-secretary for Ireland, Thomas Drummond, was appointed. A complete change in the administration of Dublin Castle under Drummond gave O'Connell hope that his policy of cooperation with the Whig government was working. In his five years in office in Ireland, Drummond reorganised the police force and encouraged Catholics to join it. He brought the appointment of local magistrates under the control of Dublin Castle, thus taking the appointments from the power of local landlords and giving the magistrates more independence. He got rid of judges who favoured one religion over another. He ended the practice of having only Protestants on juries for cases the state was presenting. He also checked the power of the Orange order by prohibiting its parades, sacking magistrates who favoured it, and so forth.

Drummond did not believe that the way to rule Ireland was with the iron fist. When a prominent landlord was murdered in 1838 and the magistrates demanded more repressive laws, Drummond said the laws were quite adequate to deal with the situation, and he laid the blame for the disturbances on the landlords who down through the years had neglected their tenants and brought the troubles on themselves. Nevertheless, Drummond used his police force well, and brought more criminals into court than ever before. Dublin Castle was improving. Alas, many other things in Ireland were not.

O'Connell was unhappy with the act passed in 1838 to end tithes, because even though the landlord now had responsibility for the tithes, the tenant farmer still had to pay them as part of his rent. O'Connell had two other main grievances: the government's treatment of the poor and its failure to reform local government in Ireland although it had been reformed in England. The new Irish poor law introduced into Parliament in 1838 was not to O'Connell's liking.

The British government had been under pressure to do something about the Irish poor since before the union in 1800; finally, it had decided that something should be done. A new Act to help the poor had been introduced in 1833 in England, and the government had appointed a commission to look at the position in Ireland. It was not until 1836 that the commission reported to the British government.

Meanwhile, the new English law had introduced a system of workhouses all over England. The Irish commission had been told that it should recommend doing the same in Ireland. It refused to listen, however, and reported that the English system would not work at all in Ireland; what was needed was something entirely different. The cause of poverty in Ireland was unemployment, said the commission, and this could be combated by an extensive scheme of public works for the development of natural resources.

The commission's report was ignored, and a new man was appointed to look at the position in Ireland. He came back and told the government what it wanted to hear: that the English system of workhouses should be extended to Ireland. This proposal was incorporated into an Act signed by the queen in July 1838.

Workhouses

The workhouses were set up in 130 places. They were run by a Board of Guardians and were paid for by a tax from the landlords and the tenant farmers. They were made as uncomfortable as possible to keep all but those in dire need from going into them. Husbands were separated from wives, brothers were separated from sisters, and children were separated from parents. Only two meals a day were served – a breakfast of seven ounces of oatmeal and a pint of buttermilk, and a dinner of three pounds of potatoes and a pint of buttermilk. No alcohol, tobacco or tea was allowed, and meals were eaten in strict silence.

O'Connell's other grievance – the failure of the government to reform local government – was a striking example of the need to repeal the union. Local government in England and Scotland had been reformed in 1834, but despite a report on the

Irish local authorities in 1835 showing them to be badly in need of reform, it was 1840 before the British did anything. The report showed that though theoretically open to Catholics since 1793, the sixty-eight city and borough corporations had in fact been dominated by Protestants all that time. Very few of the authorities in Ireland were properly elected, and most of them performed few of the functions normal to local authorities.

Finally, in 1840, the Irish Municipal Corporation Act was passed. Fifty-eight of the sixty-eight local authorities were dissolved. The remaining ten became elected councils. But the British did not give as much freedom in the election procedure as they had given in England and Scotland. In England and Scotland, every ratepayer had a vote, but in Ireland only householders paying £10 or over had one. The powers of the councils were much more limited than those of the British councils; they did not have power over the police and did not elect sheriffs. The viceroy nominated them instead.

The passing of the Act did, however, allow O'Connell the triumph of becoming the first Catholic lord mayor of Dublin since the reign of James II over a hundred years before. On becoming lord mayor in

November 1841, he declared that if the union of Ireland and England was a reality, then the British government should treat Ireland in the same way as England. The fact that it took them six years longer to do something about Irish local government proved that the only solution for Ireland was a parliament of her own.

He had tried straightforward methods of getting justice for Ireland, using all the means open to him as a Member of Parliament. He had helped to bring down the Tory government. He had worked with the Whig government, and it had disappointed him. Now, as the 1830s ended, he was convinced that the only way of getting things done was to rouse and organise the people, as he had done for Catholic emancipation. He formed a new Repeal Association in April 1840, the same month that saw the death of the undersecretary for Ireland, Thomas Drummond.

It was to be O'Connell's last great campaign, and it was to fail.

The Last Campaign

The massive public campaign for repeal of the union was the climax of O'Connell's efforts since his first appearance in public life in 1800. Then, he had opposed the Catholic powers who conspired with the British government to bring about the union. Ever since then, he had campaigned for repeal. When he began his campaign for Catholic emancipation, he intended to follow it with one for repeal. Since entering Parliament in 1830, all his energy had been devoted to it. A bill for repeal brought before the House of Commons in 1834 had been overwhelmingly defeated by 523 votes to 38. Now he saw that his constitutional approach had not worked.

O'Connell again decided to rouse the public. He announced that his new Repeal Association would be identical to the old Catholic Association. The entire population would be enrolled as associate members, contributing a penny a month. Once again, the clergy were to act as agents for the collections. In place of Bishop Doyle (now dead), O'Connell hoped for the support of Archbishop MacHale of Tuam. He contacted as many as possible of his Protestant supporters, and even persuaded one of them to act as chairman of the first meeting of the new association in the Corn Exchange buildings.

For all his organising ability, the first meeting was disappointing. Only a hundred people attended, and despite O'Connell's impassioned speech, only fifteen enrolled in the new association. His enemies watched the beginning of the new association with contempt. They felt that O'Connell at sixty-five was too old to organise a massive public campaign. There were no young leaders to help him. His friends now had good jobs with the government. Richard Shiel was a cautious senior barrister. O'Loghlen was master of the rolls. The burden of organising the campaign fell on O'Connell himself, and progress was slow.

The British Parliament was dissolved in July 1841, and a general election was called. Few people in Ireland still had the right to vote, and the Tories won heavily in Ireland, as they did in England. O'Connell's old enemy Peel became the prime minister, and in his Cabinet were many more old enemies: Wellington, Stanley, Hardinge and others.

O'Connell was elected a Member of Parliament for Cork. He was also lord mayor of Dublin. Official duties left him little time to do much about the agitation for repeal.

Nevertheless, O'Connell's speeches had their effect, and the repeal movement began to grow. He told the people at many meetings around the country that the restoration of an Irish Parliament to Dublin would solve their problems. He promised the tenant farmers protection from the landlords, the poor a better poor law, and industry protection from foreign competition.

Among the many people influenced by O'Connell were some young men of the middle classes, including Thomas Davis, a Protestant. While studying at Trinity College, he met a young Catholic from Mayo, John Blake Dillon. Both were interested in politics, and they got a chance to express that interest when they met a young journalist, Charles Gavan Duffy, a Catholic from Monaghan. All three admired O'Connell and were as anxious as he was for repeal, but they felt that the Irish people would have to be educated first. They decided on the method for doing this one autumn day in Phoenix Park and the result was the appearance, on 15 October 1842, of a new weekly newspaper, *The Nation*.

The Nation

The founders of *The Nation* were different from O'Connell's old supporters in the Catholic Association. They openly sought separation from England. O'Connell wanted to restore the Irish Parliament under the British crown, but they wanted a separate, free Ireland. Through their newspaper, they instilled in the Irish people a pride in their history, their literature, their music and their songs. They retold the old Irish legends and encouraged the use of the Irish language.

The Nation printed news reports and Irish ballads. Besides encouraging the Irish to have pride in their past, it actively campaigned for justice in the present. It demanded protection for tenants against their landlords, asked Irishmen to support Irish industry by buying Irish goods, and urged Catholics and Protestants to unite in the cause of national independence.

The Nation cost sixpence – the average daily wage of a labourer – so very few people could afford to buy it. Nonetheless, it became popular; when one man in a village bought it, he would pass it on. Or the local priest or schoolteacher might read it to the villagers.

The influence of *The Nation* was enormous, and the young men who ran it were a tremendous help to O'Connell in organising the Repeal Association around the country. These young men became known as Young Irelanders.

O'Connell felt that progress towards repeal was as inevitable as the progress towards Catholic emancipation had been. But there were important differences: the forty-shilling freeholders no longer had votes to bring him and his repealers into Parliament, and Protestant opinion in Ireland and in England was against repeal. Nevertheless, by 1843 O'Connell felt the time was ripe for the great push. He toured the south and the midlands, addressing vast crowds. He made a four-hour speech to Dublin Corporation, and won the support of forty-one members out of fifty-six.

But Peel, the prime minister, was determined to

oppose O'Connell's new agitation. In May 1843 he dismissed O'Connell and other repealers from their positions as magistrates. The result, however, was that more Protestants joined the repeal movement, including Grattan's son, William Smith O'Brien and Lord Cloncurry. O'Connell set up rival courts all around the country, to which people flocked. These courts were less expensive than the state-run ones. Even Protestant magistrates who worked in state courts supported the repeal courts by acting as unofficial magistrates.

At this crucial stage, the differences between the Young Irelanders and O'Connell and his supporters became more marked. The Young Irelanders regarded O'Connell's speeches as old fashioned, disliked his refusal to consider a completely independent Ireland, and resented his insistence on achieving repeal without violence.

The prime minister watched anxiously as O'Connell's meetings attracted larger and larger crowds. They were 'monster' meetings, and at each of them O'Connell's great voice thundered to the assembled masses. Spaced through these vast crowds were leaders of the repeal movement, who repeated what O'Connell had just said using his gestures and his method of speech. The world watched in awe as he showed how he could control these meetings. Though hundreds of thousands gathered to hear him, there was never any disorder.

Learning of the huge crowds and receiving reports of the speeches, the prime minister warned that he would risk civil war to suppress the agitation for repeal. O'Connell answered his threat at a monster meeting in Mullingar, where over 150,000 attended:

> *I want three million repealers to enrol themselves in the Association. They will be all the more dreaded by their enemies because every member will represent a man with two clenched fists.*

But the prime minister was not impressed, and repeatedly told Parliament of his unwillingness to grant repeal. O'Connell constantly reminded his audiences of the bloodless victory won for Catholic emancipation, and told them that this prime minister would have to repeal the union. But the prime minister was waiting for an opportune moment to strike at the Repeal Association.

Over 300,000 people gathered to hear O'Connell in Kilkenny. He told them that even Wellington never had such an army. A week later, an even larger crowd gathered in Mallow. This was the only time he used language that could be interpreted as encouraging violence. He told them:

> *You are the finest people on God's earth; the most moral, the most temperate, the most religious in the world, no government will dare to crush your loyal and constitutional agitation.*

That night at dinner, he went further, and spoke of his fears:

> *The time has come when we must be doing. Gentlemen you may soon have the alternative to live as slaves or die as free men. In the midst of peace and tranquillity the Saxons are covering our land with troops. The population of nine millions will not allow itself to be trampled on.*

O'Connell's threat was deliberate. He hoped to intimidate the British government, then planning repressive legislation. The monster meetings continued through the summer. One of the largest was held at Tara. At nine o'clock that morning, a small train of private carriages containing O'Connell and a dozen friends set out from Merrion Square. As it passed through the city, eager spectators occupied the windows and pavements. At various points along the way, long lines of vehicles – carriages, side-cars, wagons – were waiting to join in, and over 1,300 of them left Dublin.

The procession passed through villages and towns, and in each place the entire population turned out in their holiday dress. Their houses were decorated with banners or evergreens. In each place, too, the local band stood at the head of a long line of farm carts, ready to join the great procession. Before O'Connell had arrived within a dozen miles of Tara, he met huge crowds who had come from distant places and had camped out in the fields on that fine August night. He was thrilled to see the repealers of An Uaimh (Navan), Kells and Trim join the procession with their banners and their bands. Three miles from Tara, they had to abandon their vehicles and continue on foot, such was the crowd. The bands amounted to forty, and the banners were past counting. The whole district was covered with men and women who had from day-break till noon flocked towards O'Connell's meeting place.

The Hill of Tara rises out of a level plain. On and around it gathered probably the largest crowd ever assembled in one place in Ireland. *The Times* of London estimated that there was one million people present that afternoon.

Each week, another meeting was held. Finally, organisers set out to hold the largest monster meeting ever at Clontarf, near Dublin, where Brian Boru had driven the Danes from Ireland. It was to be the final great meeting and would show the prime minister that O'Connell could summon a peaceful army and that the Irish people wanted repeal. It was to be held on 8 October 1843. Preparations were intense. People from all over the country were converging on Dublin to attend, and a group of 1,500 came from Britain.

The prime minister saw his opportunity to strike. Until then, the government had been unable to use troops effectively near the monster meetings, but now that O'Connell was to hold one just outside Dublin, the prime minister thought it was time to call O'Connell's bluff.

There were thousands of troops at the ready in Dublin. Warships of the British navy stood at anchor off the coast near Clontarf. Artillery was moved to a position where it could control all the entrances to Clontarf. The prime minister told Dublin Castle to ban the meeting.

Meanwhile, the Repeal Association continued preparations. A huge platform was erected at Clontarf for the speakers. Neither the Repeal Association nor the thousands coming to the meeting knew of Dublin

Castle's plans. All believed that no government could shoot down thousands of people gathered together peacefully.

The Repeal Association met every day to make final arrangements. No news of the government's ban had come when the association met on Saturday 7 October, but while they were meeting, the ban was proclaimed. O'Connell immediately cancelled the Clontarf meeting. He ordered that the platform be taken down and that messengers be sent out on every road to meet the crowds and to tell them.

His long-standing belief that not one drop of blood should be shed for the cause of Ireland meant that O'Connell could make no other decision. Many people were disappointed, but the majority kept their belief in him and thought he could outwit Peel. He felt that the cancellation was only a minor setback.

When the weekly meeting of the Repeal Association was held, he denounced the ban, saying it was unconstitutional. He did not know what further action the prime minister would take, but he did not have to wait long.

The following Saturday, O'Connell, his son, two members of the Repeal Association, and the editors of the three nationalist newspapers were arrested.

They were charged with conspiring to undermine the constitution and stir dissatisfaction in the army.

O'Connell was relieved, for he thought they might be charged with high treason, a crime carrying the death penalty. The conspiracy charge, he felt, would be easy to defeat, but he underestimated the determination of the prime minister, who instructed Dublin Castle to make sure of a conviction. The old practice of keeping Catholics off the jury was ruthlessly employed. O'Connell, having managed a postponement of the trial until January, went home to Derrynane and spent the time pleasantly hunting on the mountains.

But January came, and he had to face his trial.

Imprisonment

O'Connell and his friends faced a completely Protestant and hostile jury. Everyone in court noticed the change in O'Connell. He was older; his voice was no longer strong – he did not speak with the same authority. The verdict was inevitable, and the repeal leaders were found guilty.

The judge – an old colleague of O'Connell's on the Munster circuit – told him he was to go to prison for a year and was also fined £2,000.

The prime minister had won. The English public and the opposition party, though horrified at the methods used in getting convictions, knew that they could do nothing, for the Tories had a safe majority in the House of Commons.

O'Connell now wished to disband the Repeal Association, but the Young Irelanders stopped him. He did, however, put an end to the repeal courts, and he persuaded the editors of the nationalist newspapers to resign.

The repeal leaders were not treated like ordinary prisoners. They were allowed to choose their prison, and they went to Richmond Jail. O'Connell was permitted to stay with his son in the governor's house; two of his daughters came to live with them. Soon, a stream of visitors began to come.

Though O'Connell had made up his mind that he would be in prison for a year, people in England advised him to make an appeal to the House of Lords. The action was taken, and a skilful case was presented. It was said that the jury had been wrongly chosen and that the actions of which he had been accused were not in fact against the law. The Law Lords upheld the appeal and quashed the sentence. O'Connell and his friends were released in September.

He was astonished, as he had only spent three months in jail. It seemed he had defeated Peel again. He was released from prison, but when his supporters found out that he was already at home, they arranged for him to return to jail for one further night so that they could organise a triumphal procession.

By morning, most of Dublin had gathered to watch O'Connell leave Richmond Jail. Wearing his great cape and green velvet cap, he travelled in a huge chariot made for the occasion, and all Dublin turned out to welcome him.

Everyone waited to see if he would continue the fight. But when people saw him, they knew he was no longer the man he had been. The tall man who had spoken at the monster meetings was now limp and unsteady; his deep-blue eyes had grown tired. He was now sixty-nine years old, and a lifetime of hard work and constant pressure had taken its toll.

Meanwhile, Robert Peel had begun a new policy. He thought that the British government could never achieve peace unless it could attract the support of the Catholic middle classes. He therefore made extra money available to Maynooth seminary, increasing the annual government payment from £9,000 to £26,000, and giving a special grant of £30,000 to the college for expansion. He also set up a number of new university colleges in Ireland – open to both Catholics and Protestants.

The University of Dublin (Trinity College) had been the only university in Ireland, and Peel thought that by setting up others, he could develop a well-educated middle class to oppose the political influence of agitators like O'Connell. The bill to establish these colleges was passed in the House of Commons in

1845. In 1849 the 'queen's colleges' opened in Belfast, Cork and Galway.

O'Connell and Archbishop MacHale opposed the setting up of these colleges, and called them godless colleges. The issue split the Repeal Association, and the Young Irelanders refused to allow O'Connell to campaign against the colleges through the association. They supported colleges that were open to people of different religions. Thomas Davis wrote in *The Nation*:

> *The reasons for separate education are reasons for separate life, for mutual hatred, for penal laws, for religious wars. Let those who insist on separate education follow out their principles to the end – let them prohibit Protestant boys from playing with Catholic boys, let them forbid them from talking, from walking together, let them establish a separate police force for each and let them rail off each sect into a separate quarter.*

There could never be any compromise between such beliefs and those of O'Connell.

Then, too, there was the possibility of a change in government in Britain again. The Whigs might come back into power and O'Connell wanted to cooperate with them. The Young Irelanders despised him for this, and clashed with him on the subject of physical force. He refused to acknowledge that a man should die for his country, but the Young Irelanders – though aware that Ireland was in no condition to fight – did not want to rule out the possibility of a rebellion some time in the future.

It is probable that the breach between O'Connell and the Young Irelanders would never have happened if the most able of their leaders, Thomas Davis, had not died at the age of thirty-one in September 1845. The following year, O'Connell announced that he was going to cooperate with the Whigs, and brought before the Repeal Association a resolution that it never resort to force to achieve its aims. O'Connell was pleased when the Young Irelanders left the association. The Whigs, as it turned out, failed to form a government. Peel was back in power.

The Great Famine

Soon, a disaster greater than any dispute in the Repeal Association struck Ireland. In August 1845 blight had struck the potato crop in England, and by the autumn of that year, it had crossed to Ireland. But things were not hopeless. Peel brought in some corn, and though it was not distributed free, it kept prices down. He also established relief committees that collected money for the people and organised relief work on the roads. The people – used to one season of blight – were hopeful about the next year's crop. The 1845 failure had not been total, and even in some places where it was very severe, the people had still some reserves.

Robert Peel was still in power in the spring and early summer of 1846. The weather had been warm in May and June, and the potato crop was flourishing. In July of 1846 Father Theobald Matthew, travelling from Dublin to Cork, noticed that the potato crop was blooming. But when he made the return trip almost a week later, on 3 August, he saw a completely different sight: 'I beheld with sorrow one wide waste of rotting vegetation. In many places the wretched people were seated on the fences of their gardens, wringing their hands and bewailing their misfortune.'

This time the blight was widespread, and millions of people faced the prospect of starvation.

... millions of people faced the prospect of starvation

Meanwhile in England, Robert Peel's government had fallen and a new Whig government under Lord John Russell had been formed. It misunderstood the Famine, and insisted that it was not the duty of a government to feed people. It even restricted the amount of money available for relief work, and instructed merchants not to sell goods at below 'an economic price'. Irish landlords 'should take care of their own poor'.

This attitude was caused by the total ignorance of the British government about conditions in Ireland.

Most landlords had their estates mortgaged; if they had to supply famine relief, they would go bankrupt. To avoid the responsibility of providing for their tenants, many of them simply cleared their lands by wholesale evictions. Others, however, stood up to the British government, and insisted that the responsibility for relieving the Famine lay with the government. They pointed out that if it was true that Ireland was a part of the United Kingdom, then it followed that the United Kingdom should step in and help.

It took months for the new Whig government to realise that it should do something. The Irish people had to endure the harsh winter of 1846–47 with little or no aid. Eventually, in January 1847, the government decided to act. By the following summer, it had started to feed millions of people.

The Last Journey

Never was Ireland more in need of a strong leader – a spokesman for the starving poor. But Daniel O'Connell was visibly failing, and it was with a weak voice that he spoke about the Famine to the House of Commons in February 1847.

He grew very ill and was confined to bed. He felt that he was going to die, but his doctors recommended that he travel to Rome to recover his health in a warmer climate. His doctors finally prevailed on him, and early in March he set off with his friend Fitzpatrick, one of his sons, and his confessor, Father Miley.

He was in England for St Patrick's Day, and was greeted by many of his old friends and enemies. From England, he sailed to France. He passed through France, staying in Boulogne, Abbeyville and Paris. He gave a long interview to a newspaperman in Boulogne, and his French was as fluent as it had been when he was a schoolboy.

Throughout the journey in France, bad weather followed him. Rheumatism struck him in central France, and he had to stop for a rest. It was early May before they reached Italy, and though the weather was good, Daniel had become weak. On reaching Genoa, he refused to go any further. He knew he would die in Genoa, and within a few days of his arrival death did indeed seem inevitable. Congestion of the brain set in, and he became delirious.

He knew he would die in Genoa

Within a few days, he was slipping so badly that he requested the Last Sacrament. Father Miley sent word to Cardinal Archbishop of Genoa, who came at two o'clock on the morning of 15 May 1847 to give the Last Sacrament. Shortly afterwards, Daniel O'Connell died.

He had one last request – that his heart should be embalmed and taken to Rome, and that his body should be brought back to Ireland. His heart now lies in a silver urn in the Irish College in Rome; his body lies in Glasnevin Cemetery, where a round tower marks his grave.

If you look back over Irish history, you will probably find no other person who made such an impact as O'Connell. At a time when the people were downtrodden, he raised them and showed them how to defeat their conquerors. He was one of the first to realise the pressure that can be exerted on governments through public meetings and abstention from court systems. In achieving Catholic emancipation, he showed the power of the people when they speak with one voice.

Also in the Series...

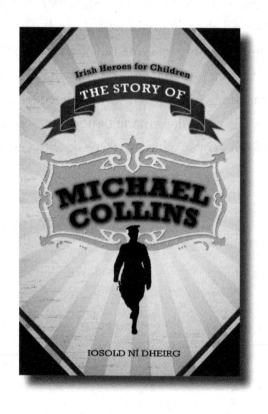